MONTEZUMA
AND THE
AZTECS

Nathaniel Harris

Illustrated by Gerry Wood

The Bookwright Press
New York · 1986

LIFE AND TIMES

Alexander the Great and the Greeks
Julius Caesar and the Romans
Alfred the Great and the Saxons
Canute and the Vikings
William the Conqueror and the Normans
Richard the Lionheart and the Crusades
Columbus and the Age of Exploration
Montezuma and the Aztecs
Elizabeth I and Tudor England
Daniel Boone and the American West

Further titles are in preparation.

First published in the United States in 1986 by
The Bookwright Press
387 Park Avenue South
New York, NY 10016

First published in 1985 by
Wayland (Publishers) Ltd
61 Western Road, Hove
East Sussex BN3 1JD, England

© Copyright 1985 Wayland (Publishers) Ltd

Second impression 1986

ISBN 0-531-18028-X

Library of Congress Catalog Card Number 85-71724

Phototypeset by Planagraphic Typesetters Ltd
Printed by G. Canale & C.S.p.A., Turin, Italy

Contents

1 MONTEZUMA, THE UNLUCKY EMPEROR

"Master of Cuts"

For many centuries, Europeans had no idea that such a place as the Americas existed. Then, in 1492, Christopher Columbus took three Spanish ships across the Atlantic Ocean and reached the islands of the Caribbean. He believed that he had arrived at India, and therefore called the natives "Indians."

These natives of Central and South America lived in all sorts of societies, including a number of very advanced civilizations. By Columbus's time, most of Central America had come to be dominated by a single mighty empire — the empire of the Aztecs, ruled by Montezuma II.

As a child, Montezuma had been carefully educated as a possible future emperor. In special schools, Montezuma and other nobles went through a religious training which included fasting, prayer, and cutting and piercing their own flesh — for blood played a leading role in Aztec religion. He learned to read Aztec picture-writing and to understand their complicated calendar. At the age of eighteen he became a seasoned warrior — a "Master of Cuts" — by capturing enemies alive in battle. On the death of his uncle in 1503, he was elected emperor.

Above *The Aztecs had no alphabet. They wrote in pictures, or glyphs. An Aztec book was a colorful jumble of pictures which told a story. This glyph represents Montezuma.*

Opposite *The Aztecs were a warrior race, so all young men had to learn the skills of warfare. Here Montezuma is using a wooden sword and shield to fight an opponent. The weapons they used in battle were far more deadly (see page 15).*

Lord of the Aztecs

At the start of 1519, the Emperor Montezuma II seemed a man to be envied. He was the most powerful ruler in Central America, controlling territories that stretched from the Atlantic to the Pacific Ocean. Most of this large area now forms part of the modern state of Mexico, which is named after the Aztecs, who were also known as the Mexica. Montezuma seemed to have had nothing to fear from enemies, for the only other great empire in that part of the world — that of the Incas — was two thousand miles away on the west coast of South America.

The Aztecs were enriched by their successes in war. They forced the peoples they conquered to send them lavish tributes in the form of food and other materials. So the Aztec nobles and their emperor lived in pomp and splendor, wore rich jewelry and fantastically designed feathered costumes, and enjoyed a way of life that was, in many respects, highly civilized.

Proud as his nobles were, they humbled themselves before Montezuma. The emperor was treated as if he were a god. Two hundred chieftains lived in his palace and served as his bodyguard, but most of them were not even allowed to speak to him. Before coming into his presence, they had to take off their fine robes and put on common clothes. They also had to go barefoot, and keep their eyes lowered, since it was forbidden to look upon the emperor's face. They were grateful if he spoke to them, and left his chamber reverently, backing away from him. The rest of the people rarely saw this god-like being, except on great ceremonial occasions. Yet Montezuma, who seemed all-powerful, was a frightened man.

Above *The mask of the god Quetzalcoatl. At a royal burial ceremony it was placed over the face of the dead emperor.*

Opposite *When Montezuma II became emperor in 1503, he was treated like a god. When he was carried through the streets on a litter, everyone had to lower their eyes to the ground, on pain of death.*

Fear of the future

Above *The figure of the god Quetzalcoatl rises from the jaws of a feathered serpent.*

Montezuma was neither a coward nor a fool. He had proved that he was, by the cruel standards of his time, an able ruler. He had crushed a rebellion so thoroughly that twelve thousand prisoners had been taken and sacrificed to the Aztec war god, Huitzilopochtli. He had fully revenged himself on an ally who had murdered his sister, and he had made his authority felt far and wide among the peoples who paid tribute to the Aztecs.

But Montezuma's mind was disturbed by religious fears. All sorts of signs appeared to be threatening his empire with doom. A comet was seen making its fiery way across the sky. Temples burst into flames. There were sudden floods, and it was said that a woman's voice could

be heard in the night, telling people to run away from their chief city, Tenochtitlán.

Even more alarming were reports that reached Montezuma from the coast, far away to the east. These told him that strange, pale, bearded men had arrived from the sea, carried on mysterious floating islands.

Montezuma had no way of knowing that the newcomers were Spaniards who had crossed the Atlantic Ocean from Europe, or that their "islands" were actually wooden ships. What he did know was that one of his gods, Quetzalcoatl, was white and bearded. According to Aztec legend, this god had sailed away to the east, but had promised to return one day. If the pale, bearded beings turned out to be Quetzalcoatl and his followers, Montezuma and his people would be duty-bound to submit to them and obey them in all things.

Above *Although Montezuma was the all-powerful leader of a great empire, omens — a fiery comet and temples bursting into flames — warned him that something terrible was about to happen.*

The "white gods"

Reports about the "white gods" — the Spaniards — became even more frightening. They were mounted on strange beasts like deer, which snorted, foamed at the mouth, and thudded over the ground with a tremendous noise. When the strangers were angry, they could kill men at a distance with sticks that flamed and smoked. No wonder the Aztecs were terrified: they had never before seen horses, cannons or firearms.

Were the strangers gods or ordinary men? Montezuma remained uncertain. He sent them food and gifts, but he also told his sorcerers to cast spells on them. To his dismay, Aztec magic seemed to have no effect.

When the Spaniards began to march on his capital, Montezuma first ordered them to stop, and then offered to pay them an annual tribute. But still they advanced. Finally, Montezuma arranged an ambush — but it went disastrously wrong. Pretending to know nothing about it, the emperor decided to welcome the apparently unstoppable Spaniards to his city.

Montezuma soon discovered that they were anything but godlike, for they seized him and held him as a hostage. This final blow seems to have broken Montezuma's spirit. He prevented his nobles from attacking the Spaniards, and agreed to become a vassal of Spain. When the Aztecs did rebel, he tried to restore peace.

By this time, Montezuma's own people had lost faith in him. When he appeared before them, he was showered with stones and spears. According to the Spaniards, he died of the wounds he received, although it is also possible that they murdered him. So perished the unlucky emperor.

Above *A gold piece of jewelry shows Mixtantecutli, god of death.*

Opposite *The terrible thing that had been predicted was the coming of the Spaniards in 1519. It is probable that Montezuma was killed by his own people when he made peace with the Spaniards.*

2 WHO WERE THE AZTECS?

Above *Before they finally settled in the Valley of Mexico, the Aztecs had been a wandering people. Often they were forced to move on by hostile natives from other tribes.*

The Aztecs dominated their empire from their cities in the Valley of Mexico. This was a pleasant fertile area surrounding a large lake. It lay at the heart of Mexico's cool central plateau, high above the hot and wet tropical lowlands.

The valley had been the home of civilized peoples for at least a thousand years before the Aztecs entered it. They were semi-barbarians who appeared out of the barren northwest in the thirteenth century. Since there were already many people in the valley, the Aztecs were not welcome, and they were driven from place to place.

The Aztecs finally took refuge in the swamps and islands of the lake itself. This proved an excellent choice, since the lake provided plenty of food and the site was easy to defend. In time, the swamps and islands were transformed into the great city of Tenochtitlán.

The Aztecs paid tribute to the ruling people in the valley, the Tepanecs, until 1428, when they allied with two other subject peoples and crushed their overlords. Within a few years the Aztecs had become the dominant partners in this alliance and were conquering in all directions. They adopted the civilization of the peoples they had subdued, and burned the records of their own early, humble history. By the reign of Montezuma II, their empire was the largest ever seen in Central America, and the Aztec warrior seemed invincible.

Below   *The map shows Tenochtitlán on Lake Texcoco, the capital of the Aztec Empire. It also shows the routes taken by Cortés and the Spanish army in their rapid conquest of the Aztecs in 1519-21.*

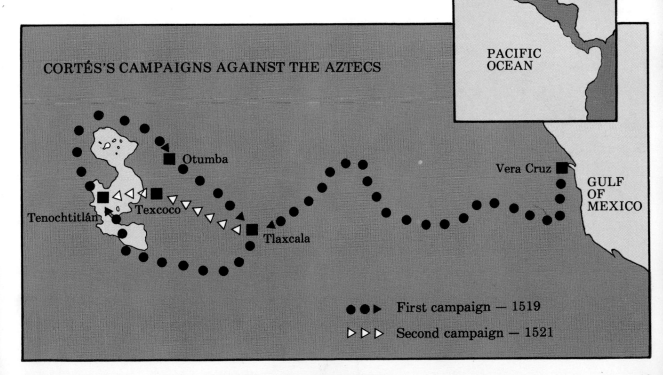

PACIFIC OCEAN

CORTÉS'S CAMPAIGNS AGAINST THE AZTECS

Otumba

Vera Cruz

GULF OF MEXICO

Tenochtitlán

Texcoco

Tlaxcala

● ● ▶   First campaign — 1519

▷ ▷ ▷   Second campaign — 1521

13

3 THE AZTEC EMPIRE

Below *The Aztecs believed that the souls of warriors who died in battle went to a special heaven near the sun.*

Warrior race

The Aztecs were constantly at war, making new conquests and putting down rebellions. Yet, unlike most empire-builders, they had no permanent professional army to patrol borders and march anywhere at a moment's notice. An Aztec army consisted of all the male citizens who were needed for any particular campaign. In boyhood they had been trained as warriors, and so almost every able-bodied man expected to leave his fields and fight, when called on by the leader of his clan. They had

little fear of death because they believed that when a warrior died in battle, his soul went to a special heaven near the sun.

The army's equipment was stored in special places and only handed out when the men were ready to march. The Aztecs had no iron, so their weapons were made from wood, tipped with obsidian. They used spears which they sometimes propelled from an atlatl, or wooden thrower, bows and arrows, and "swords" which were more like spiked clubs. They seem primitive to us today but they would have been quite effective against a foe who was similarly armed. Quilted cotton armor and wicker shields were the Aztec's main defensive equipment. Since they had no horses or pack animals, they marched everywhere on foot, carrying their own gear. It is surprising that they managed to campaign so successfully even when several hundred miles from their homes.

With such limited equipment, it was probably more common for warriors to be wounded in battle than to be killed outright. But this fitted in very well with Central American ideas about warfare.

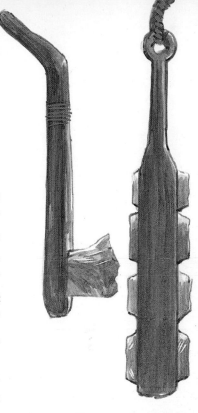

Above *Two wooden clubs, spiked with obsidian.*

Below *Weapons of war — a shield, a spear — a glyph of blue Humming Bird, one of the four representations of the god of war and sun god — Huitzilopochtli.*

Aztec knights

Although the Aztecs had no professional army, there were groups of crack fighting soldiers among them who may have been more or less full-time soldiers. They seem to have been organized on similar lines to the knightly orders of medieval Europe, with special duties and their own ritual dances and ceremonies. The two main orders, the Eagle Knights and the Jaguar Knights, wore battledress partly made from the skins of the animals whose names they had taken. Since they often put on wooden helmets with their insignia carved on them, they had what were in effect uniforms.

Other units had similar means of distinguishing between friends and foes in the heat of battle, and an Aztec army must have been a colorful sight. Experienced warriors with good war records were allowed to dress more extravagantly than their fellows. The commanders were the most striking figures of all, carrying on their backs wooden frames that were hung with great wreaths of featherwork designs. It is hard to believe they can have fought very energetically without spoiling their plumage!

The most honored of Aztec warriors were not those who slew many enemies, but those who took most prisoners. So in battle the soldier aimed to wound, or disarm, rather than kill an opponent. The Aztecs' enemies behaved in the same way. This odd situation arose because the peoples of Central America believed that their gods demanded human sacrifices on a vast scale; so the only way to satisfy them was to deliver thousands of captives to the sacrificial altars. In the Aztec world, then, war and religion were linked — and religion was responsible for the greater horrors.

Opposite *Prisoners of war wait to be sacrificed in the Great Temple.*

Right *Jaguar Knights and Eagle Knights were the crack troops of the Aztec army.*

Cactus City

Above   *When the Aztecs were looking for a homeland, the gods said they must build their city on the spot where they first saw an eagle sitting on a cactus on a rock. This glyph is of Tenochtitlán, which means "Cactus City."*

The capital of the Aztecs' empire was Tenochtitlán, which can be roughly translated as "Cactus City." When the Spaniards first saw it, in 1519, they were dazzled, and exclaimed that they must be enchanted or dreaming. Approaching, they saw prosperous towns lining the lakeside, and the brilliant blue water thronged with canoes. Three long causeways stretched from the shore all the way across the water to the capital. But the greatest wonder was the city itself, with its glittering stone buildings apparently rising straight up out of the lake.

Tenochtitlán began as a group of settlements built on islands, but it was constantly enlarged over its two centuries of existence. Thousands of stakes were driven into the bed of the lake to provide solid bases for new houses. Other techniques of land reclamation were used to create large floating gardens where Aztec farmers would tend crops. As a result, Tenochtitlan had become a city in which the main "roads" were a network of canals. Anyone who wished to go far would travel by canoe, which was convenient in a land without horses or other beasts of burden.

About two hundred thousand people lived in Tenochtitlán, and there were many fine houses. But it was, above all, a city of temples and palaces. At its heart, the Wall of Serpents enclosed the pyramid-temples of the chief gods, with their bloodstained altars. Nearby lay the emperor's palace, from which the Aztec state was governed. Across the causeways or in canoes, the city received the rewards of greatness — the products of trade and the tribute of subject peoples.

Opposite   *Tenochtitlán, the Aztec's capital city, was built on an island in the middle of Lake Texcoco. They built canals, instead of roads, among the shallow swamps of the island. You can see the causeways that joined the island to the mainland.*

Trade and tribute

When the Aztecs defeated an enemy, they captured as many prisoners as they could, but they did not try to occupy or destroy the conquered kingdom. They were content to receive a heavy tribute from it — a tribute that became still heavier if the subject people dared to rebel.

In Montezuma's time, huge quantities of foodstuffs, as well as luxury items such as elaborate featherwork cloaks, jade and gold, poured into Tenochtitlán from all over the empire. The variety of tribute was so great that civil servants had to keep detailed accounts of goods owed and received; and some Aztec record books still survive today.

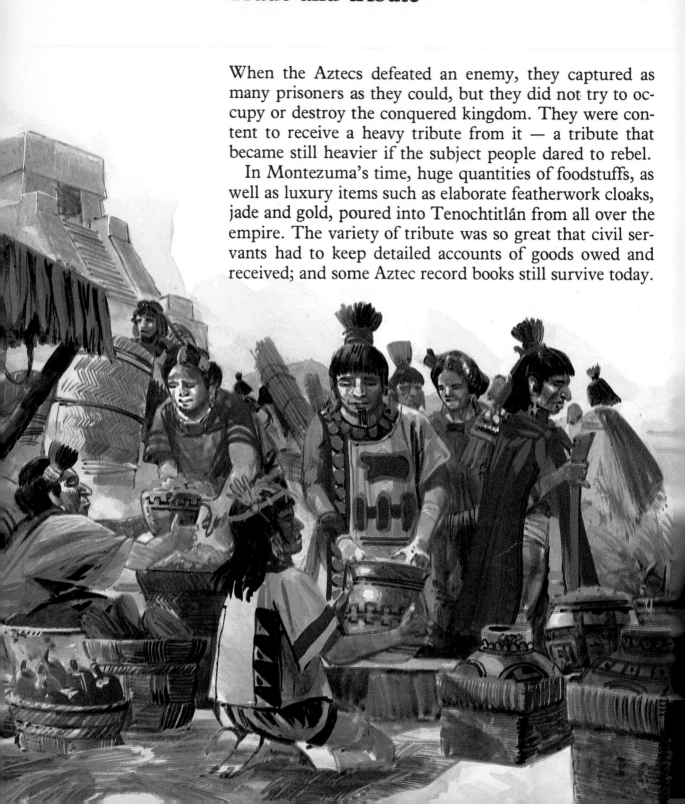

Apart from the emperor himself, the nobility probably benefited most from the tribute system. But so too did the ordinary people who flocked to large local markets — like the splendid Tlatelolco market — where they could find everything from fish and fruit to slaves and animal skins. Most deals were carried out by barter. Any difference in value between the objects being bartered was made up with cacao beans, little packets of gold dust or copper axes — which served as primitive forms of money.

All forms of commerce were tightly controlled by the Aztec authorities, and long-distance trade was made to serve their political ambitions. Specially trained merchants, the pochteca, did business with the independent peoples outside the empire, and also spied on them very efficiently. When the pochteca had done their work, the Aztecs would declare war and fight to add another unwilling territory to their empire.

Below *The market at Tlatelolco was a bustling and lively place, well stocked with merchandise from all over Central America.*

Emperor and Snake Woman

Above *Montezuma often received tribute from the subjects of his empire. Standing by him is Snake Woman — the second most important person in the Aztec Empire — who was in fact a man.*

The emperor of the Aztecs was chosen by the leading men of the realm. In practice their choice was restricted to members of a single royal family, and they selected an experienced and mature adult. A child ruler would have been unthinkable, since an emperor had to be both a war chief and a religious leader.

Once chosen, the emperor had absolute power. One reason why the Spaniards met with so little opposition was that the Aztecs continued to obey Montezuma even after he had become a prisoner. Disobedience would have been a sin as well as a crime. The emperor not only presided over great religious events: he was himself holy — so holy that he was normally carried everywhere in a

litter so that his feet never touched the common ground.

The next highest officer in the empire was the Snake Woman. The holder of this curious title was in fact a man, and a member of the royal family. At one period of Aztec history the Snake Woman seems to have been "the power behind the throne," making all the important decisions in the name of the emperor. By Montezuma's time there was no doubt that the emperor really did rule, but the Snake Woman did stand in for him on some occasions, and often became his successor.

Below the Snake Woman came a council of four, which included the two generals-in-chief of the army, backed up by a variety of other councilors and state officers. Since the provinces consisted mainly of tribute-paying subject peoples who governed themselves, the only important imperial officers were the Aztec tax collectors.

4 THE AZTEC WAY OF LIFE

Aztec society

There was little room for change in the Aztec world. Most people stayed in the same social position throughout their lives. Each class had to dress, behave and even cut its hair in a particular manner, and the penalty for disobedience was death.

The most privileged order, the nobility, owned most of the land. All the important political and military leaders were nobles. Priests also came from the nobility, and received an exclusive education in religious knowledge,

law and mathematics at special schools that were closed to ordinary boys.

Within the nobility, a man's standing depended on the number of captives he had taken. There had to be at least four of these if he was to be recognized as a fullfledged warrior, entitled to wear a distinctive orange cloak with a striped border. Occasionally a man was promoted to the nobility as a reward for his valor in battle, but since this rarely happened it seems likely that noble commanders usually took the credit for the exploits of their men.

Merchants formed the second most important class — many of them were in fact more wealthy than some of the nobles — and they sometimes formed their own army units. Apart from craftsmen, who were organized in guilds, the mass of the people farmed small plots or worked as laborers for richer men. At the very bottom of the social order was a relatively small number of slaves.

Below *There were only a few slaves in Aztec society. They were either criminals, prisoners of war, or people who had sold themselves into slavery. They were forced to wear uncomfortable wooden collars if they did not work hard enough or had been caught thieving.*

Above *Xochiquetzal, the flower goddess and patron of all flowering plants.*

Law and order

Above *The Aztecs punished crimes harshly. Even for the small crime of disobedience, young children were held over a fire of burning peppers to make their eyes sting.*

The Aztecs developed a legal system that was carefully thought out, although it is hard to know how well it worked in practice. Judges were paid, and were therefore forbidden on pain of death to take bribes. In addition to local courts, there was a central court at the emperor's palace at Tenochtitlán. It was generally presided over by the Snake Woman, but any difficult case was put before the emperor himself.

Throughout history, penalties for crimes have usually been severe. Most societies have not had prisons or large police forces, and so governments have tried to terrify people into obeying the law. This was just what the Aztecs did. Punishments started young: children were pricked with cactus needles or made to jump into a pool of

26

ice-cold water if they were disobedient. For adults, almost all crimes — even being drunk in a public place — were punishable by death.

The main exception to this state of affairs was theft. If the stolen items were replaceable, the thief became a slave until his labors had produced twice as much as he had taken. The victims received the full amount of their losses and the rest went to the royal treasury as a fine.

Many of the thieves must have been poor folk. We know that in hard times many people sold themselves or their children into slavery to avoid starving. So it was possible to be very poor in Aztec society, despite the quantities of tribute flowing in. However, Aztec law did make some attempt to help those who were worst off: corn and beans were sown along the edges of roadways, which could be taken by those who were on the brink of starvation.

Below *Hungry people were able to eat food that was specially planted for them on the edge of pathways.*

Above *Large teams of laborers were used to build the canals that crisscrossed Tenochtitlán.*

The fertile land

Above *Carrots and sweet potatoes: two popular Aztec crops.*

Most Aztecs were farmers. Their chief crops were nourishing and plentiful: a staple cereal, corn, a wide variety of beans, valuable for their protein, and squash. Many of their other foods, such as tomatoes, avocados and peppers, were then unknown to Europeans, though we now take them for granted. Pineapples were imported from the coastal lowlands of the southeast, an area which also supplied cacao beans. The Aztecs were passionately fond of these beans, from which they made drinking chocolate. They also had an alcoholic drink, pulque, which is still drunk in Mexico. It was made from a useful all-purpose plant, the maguey cactus, which had spikes that the Aztecs used as needles, and fibers that were made into cheap fabrics.

Meat played a small part in the Aztec diet. Until Europeans arrived, there were no horses, cattle, sheep, pigs or goats in America — which also meant that cheese, milk and butter were lacking. The Aztecs possessed only two edible domestic animals, the dog and the turkey, and deer were the only game animals of any size. Hairless dogs were thought to be a great delicacy!

Most of the Aztecs' farming techniques were primitive. Since they had no beasts of burden, they could not plow the land or transport produce and people in wagons. So the wheel was not of crucial importance to them, and was used only for children's toys. They also had no iron, and could only work the most yielding land with their spades, made from wood and obsidian. But with their great irrigation projects they partly overcame these disadvantages and succeeded in feeding a population of millions.

Above *Tomatoes and corn: two more crops grown by the Aztecs.*

Below *Farmers worked hard to cultivate crops such as corn, using wooden sticks to dig the soil.*

Aztec women

Warrior societies do not value women highly, except as mothers of future warriors. In the Aztec world, women had fewer legal rights than men, though they were allowed to own property and to divorce a cruel husband — if they could convince a male court that he *was* cruel. If a wife failed to bear children, her husband had an automatic right to divorce her.

Marriage was the only "career" open to a girl, even if she was of noble blood. The emperor and the nobility were allowed more than one wife, and many marriages were family alliances rather than love matches. Being under the thumb of a jealous Chief Wife must have been one of the less appealing sides of a noble girl's life!

Occasionally the widow of a chief seems to have wielded a certain amount of power by acting in the name of her

Below *Some Aztec women worked as healers, using many different herbs to cure illnesses.*

Above *Every social class had its own special hairstyle. Unmarried girls wore their hair loose. Married women wore their hair in braids rather like horns!*

infant son. The ordinary girl had no such chance. Soon after her birth, her parents put toy implements into her hands and guided them in the motions of spinning and weaving. Later, she went to a girls' school where she learned how to run a household. She married at sixteen, and settled down to a life of cooking, weaving, marketing, helping in the fields, and raising children. If she was fortunate, she might work as a healer using herbal medicines — but only after her children were grown up.

However, Aztec women did play a direct part in religious activities, serving as priestesses in the temples. In the Aztec heaven, the souls of the "best" women were given the privilege of helping the sun god across the sky. The most admirable quality of these women, to the Aztec way of thinking, was that they had died giving birth to future warriors.

Above *Aztec girls learned to weave at an early age using their skills to produce brightly-colored cloth.*

Sacred games

Like us, the Aztecs enjoyed sports and games, and were often prepared to bet on them. By far the most important sport was the sacred ball game, tlachtli, played with a hard rubber ball by two teams in a walled court. The game was rather like a form of basketball, with a "net" or goal of hollowed-out stone on each side wall. The players were not allowed to use their hands or feet, but struck the ball with elbows, hips or knees. There were seats in tiers for spectators, and wealthy nobles seem to have hired and bet on professional players.

The sacred ball game was not an Aztec invention. It was played all over civilized Central America, and dated back to at least 500 B.C. — which makes it the longest-lived of all ball games. One reason for its importance was its sacred character: the game was a religious event as well as a sporting one, and its outcome was prophetic. Montezuma himself is said to have put a prophecy of doom to the test by playing the ball game — and to have lost it.

Other games were also supposed to be prophetic, even the most popular board game, patolli. As so often among the Aztecs, religion and war were unpleasantly combined, even in sports. When there was no war to provide enough prisoners for sacrifice, the Aztecs and their neighbors held a mock battle, the "War of Flowers." The object of this war game was not victory but a supply of captives, whose deaths on the sacrificial altar were real enough.

Opposite *Tlachtli — a sacred ball game — was the most important sport. It was played between two teams in a walled court. The players tried to knock a hard rubber ball through a hollowed-out stone on each side wall. They were only allowed to hit the ball with elbows, hips or knees.*

Crafts and fashion

Above *The Aztecs were excellent craftsmen. Using only poor tools, sculptors carved fine stone statues. They also made beautiful pieces of jewelry out of jade or turquoise.*

Aztec cities supported thriving communities of craftsmen who were organized into guilds. Members of a particular guild all lived and worked in the same part of the city, just as they did in sixteenth-century Europe. Their products were luxury goods, since they must have worked mainly for the nobility or the state. Scribes painted books of records in Aztec picture-writing. Specialists carved in wood or stone, painted wall decorations for monuments, palaces and temples, or produced high-quality pottery.

The Aztecs liked beautiful clothes and dressed extravagantly during great ceremonies and on the battlefield. Dress also served to indicate rank. Ordinary men wore coarse loincloths and cloaks knotted at the shoulder, and ordinary women dressed in sleeveless tops covering simple, belted skirts. Thanks to the women's skill as weavers, the coarse fiber garments were colorful enough, but they could not compare with the lavishly embroidered cotton garments that only nobles were allowed to wear.

The difference was emphasized by other forms of decoration. Featherwork was a special and ancient Central American art, and the makers of dazzling headdresses and other feather objects were among the most admired craftsmen. Others worked in gold, silver and precious stones, producing ornaments that Aztec nobles wore in their ears, noses and lips. Jade was regarded as far more valuable than gold, and the most precious stone of all, the turquoise, was reserved for a single person — the emperor himself.

Above *An example of Aztec craftsmanship: this gold earring is fashioned in the shape of a skull from which hang tiny bells.*

Below *Featherworking was an important Aztec craft. The craftsmen made beautiful headdresses and other ornaments. The feathers came from very exotic birds, like the turquoise hummingbird.*

Life in the home

As soon as two people married, they set up house together. The rich and powerful lived in mansions made of stone, but most men had to build their own houses, using adobe (bricks of dried mud) strengthened with fillings of twigs. They thatched the roof or made it of timber beams plastered over with lime.

The average Aztec house consisted of two windowless ground floor rooms. In one, the "living room," the main piece of furniture was a set of reed mats on which the family sat or slept. The other was the kitchen, with a hearth sunk into the center of the earth floor.

The family rose with the sun and the man went off to

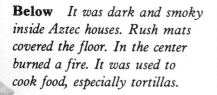

Below *It was dark and smoky inside Aztec houses. Rush mats covered the floor. In the center burned a fire. It was used to cook food, especially tortillas.*

work in the fields. His wife spent much of her time preparing and cooking meals, which was a laborious business without modern gadgets. The main food, corn, had to be freshly prepared every day by boiling, peeling and grinding it into meal so that it could be made into porridge or tortillas. The tortilla, a flat cake of unleavened bread (that is, with nothing added to make it rise), is still the staple food of Mexico. Indeed, this and many other features of the Aztecs' home life would not seem so very strange to present-day Mexican villagers.

Other jobs done in the home included spinning, weaving, making pottery and preparing pulque, the Aztecs' beer. Children were also given work to do in the home from an early age. It would seem a hard, monotonous life to most of us, but it had its compensations in the form of festivals and other colorful celebrations.

Feasts and ceremonies

The Aztecs celebrated private events, such as birthdays, by dancing to the music of flutes, rattles, drums, and vigorously blown shell-trumpets. They were great lovers of flowers, and decked themselves out with garlands. They also recited poetry which — since most of them could not read — they learned by heart.

Like so many aspects of Aztec life, public occasions were religious as well as festive events. Every month had its rituals and ceremonies — to ask for rain or celebrate its arrival, to welcome the new corn or rejoice in the harvest. The splendid processions, and the dancing and gaiety, were accompanied by the grisly but everyday sights of human sacrifices and priests wearing the skins of their victims.

One of the most spectacular Aztec ceremonies was the volador, which is still performed in parts of Mexico. It involves men, dressed as birds or gods, leaping into space from a revolving platform at the top of a high pole. Each man is fastened by a rope which is connected to the top of the pole. It unwinds as he falls, and the skillful performer can manipulte it so that he appears to fly or float to the ground.

The public ceremonies went on for three hundred and sixty days of each year. The last five days of the Aztec year were grim ones, in which people cowered in their homes, wondering whether the world was about to end. Only with the arrival of the New Year could the cycle of life safely begin again.

Opposite   *The Volador ceremony: men dressed as birds or gods, attached themselves by rope to a revolving platform at the top of a pole. As the rope unwound they appeared to float to the ground.*

5 RELIGION

Temples and shrines

When the Aztecs entered the Valley of Mexico as despised semi-barbarians, they brought with them their own tribal god, Huitzilopochtli. They took the rest of their religion from the peoples they encountered. Strange gods, human sacrifice, a complicated religious calendar and the sacred ball game: all these features of "Aztec" religion were at least two thousand years old, and were found in even the most ancient Central American civilizations.

Above *A stone sculpture of the Aztec rain god, Tlaloc.*

Below *The main square in the centre of Tenochtitlán. It shows the temples where humans were sacrificed to the Aztec gods.*

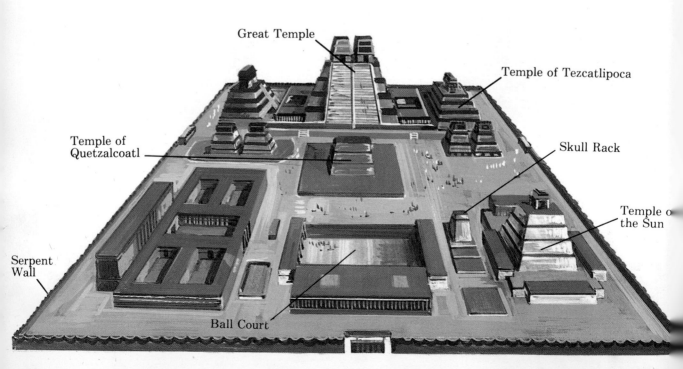

Great Temple

Temple of Tezcatlipoca

Temple of Quetzalcoatl

Skull Rack

Temple o the Sun

Serpent Wall

Ball Court

Above left *A glyph of Tlaloc, the rain god and* **above right,**
*another glyph of the god, Huitzilopochtli, who was the sun god as well
as the god of war (see page 15).*

'This was also true of the colossal pyramid temples,
whose remains are among the most impressive sights in
Central America. At the top of these temples the god had
his shrine, with an altar for human sacrifice in front of it.

The temples of Tenochtitlán were destroyed by the
Spaniards, but we do know something about them. The
city's main religious center was enclosed by a stone wall
carved in the shape of huge serpent heads. Inside lay a
great complex of buildings including three temples, a
court for the sacred ball game, and a school.

Towering over all, decorated with fantastic paintings
and carvings, was the Great Temple itself, a huge
building with a double staircase leading up to two shrines.
It was dedicated to the two gods who were most important
to the Aztecs: Huitzilopochtli, sun god, and Tlaloc, god
of the other life-giving element, the rain.

Above *At the end of each
year, the Aztecs feared that the
gods might put an end to all life.
They stayed in their homes,
waiting nervously for the dawn
of the New Year.*

The sun and stars

Above *An Aztec calendar
stone.*

There were eighteen months, each of twenty days, in the
Aztec calendar — a total of 360 days. The five remaining
days in each solar year were of evil omen. Women and
children were kept indoors, since they might otherwise be
turned into beasts or demons. As each day passed, people
became more anxious: would the gods allow the world to
go on for another year? A few hours before the end of the
last day, all fires were put out. When the altar fires were
successfully lit at the dawn of the New Year, rejoicing —
and sacrifices — were in order. The world had been saved
again.

Aztec life was full of such anxieties. The gods might
doom the world at the end of the year or, more likely, at
the end of the fifty-two year Aztec "century." Each

person's life was governed by fate and parents called upon priests to consult their almanacs to find out if their children had been born on a favorable day. If the day was unlucky, the priest might agree to falsify the records and, presumably, fool the gods.

The Aztecs studied the sky carefully, but scientifically. The most fearful event of all was acted out there: the sun's struggle to cross the sky, and to defeat the moon and stars in order tō rise again next morning. He was helped along by the souls of warriors and women who had died in childbirth. But he also needed food to give him strength, and the food of the gods was human hearts.

Below *When the New Year finally arrived priests lit fires to celebrate the saving of the world.*

The hungry gods

Apart from Huitzilopochtli, the Aztecs' tribal god, warrior god and sun god, there were many other gods who had to be honored and pacified: the most important were Tezcatlipoca, who saw into the hearts of people; Tlaloc, who brought rain for the crops; and Quetzalcoatl, the white god of creation whose return was promised.

They demanded sacrifices from the frightened Aztecs, and men, women and children were killed for them in various unpleasant ways. The commonest involved the offering of a still-beating human heart. The victim was sometimes a slave, but most often a prisoner of war. Many are said to have gone willingly to their deaths, which was regarded as the highest honor. At the climax of the ceremony, the victim danced or was carried up the steps of the pyramid and laid across an altar, where a priest skillfully slashed his chest with a flint knife and ripped out his heart. The priests sang and danced for hours during these gruesome ceremonies and yet never grew tired because the black paint covering their bodies contained a drug which gave them boundless energy.

Most peoples have practiced human sacrifice at some time. The Aztecs horrify us just because they took their beliefs so seriously. They succeeded in offering victims to the gods in huge numbers because their fighting skills were designed to obtain a steady supply of prisoners. But these very skills handicapped them when they faced an unfamiliar enemy: the Spaniards.

Opposite *In a terrifying and bloody ceremony, black-painted priests sacrifice a human to the Aztec gods. Using a flint knife, the priests rip out the still-beating heart of the victim.*

Above *A sacrificial knife with a mosaic Eagle Knight as its handle.*

Above *In 1519, Cortés and a small force of Spaniards landed at Vera Cruz on the Mexican coast. He was met by representatives of many Central American tribes, including the Tlaxcalans who became his allies against the Aztecs.*

6 THE COMING OF THE SPANIARDS

The strangers approach

In August 1519 a small force of Spaniards, led by Hernán Cortés, began their march inland from Vera Cruz towards Tenochtitlán. It was daring of them even to leave the coast, for Cortés had only about six hundred men and sixteen horses with him. Yet in two years he and his men were to overthrow an empire. They had some advantages over the Aztecs: horses, firearms and iron swords. Although they did not know it, they also had the advantage of being "gods" in the uncertain mind of Montezuma.

Hernán Cortés was a man of iron determination. He pressed on despite the fact that he had Spanish enemies who might attack him from the rear. He even ordered the boats of his expedition to be destroyed so that the Spaniards would have to conquer or die.

Cortés had two important early successes. He persuaded the coastal rulers to refuse to give tribute to Montezuma and join him. This revealed one of the Aztecs' great weaknesses: the subject peoples, condemned to pay huge tributes, would turn against them at the first opportunity. The second success was the great victory Cortés won over the Tlaxcalans, an independent people whom the Aztecs had never succeeded in conquering. The Tlaxcalans became the most loyal of Cortés's allies.

Montezuma sent the Spaniards quantities of gold, not realizing that he was merely whetting their appetite for plunder. Sorcery, ambush and half-hearted traps failed to stop the Spaniards until they reached the Aztec capital itself.

Above *The Spaniard, Hernán Cortés, conqueror of the Aztecs 1519-21.*

47

Cortés traps Montezuma

Below *After a 400 km (250 mile) march, Cortés reached Tenochtitlán. This first meeting with Montezuma was friendly. But a fight between Aztecs and Spaniards on the coast gave Cortés an excuse to make Montezuma a prisoner.*

On November 8, 1519 Montezuma met the Spaniards, who were accompanied by a large contingent of their Tlaxcalan allies. The emperor walked beneath a canopy while his nobles swept the ground in front of him and put down cloaks for him to tread on. Even so, he greeted Cortés as one who was either a god or the messenger of a god. The meeting was friendly, and the entire Spanish force was lodged in one of the royal palaces.

But within a week Cortés showed his hand. A fight between Aztecs and Spaniards, far away on the coast, gave him an excuse to act. He seized Montezuma and held him as a hostage.

For a long time the Aztecs continued to obey the emperor, even though he was doing everything the

Spaniards asked. Cortés felt confident enough to begin an attack on the Aztecs' religion, breaking into temples and smashing images of their gods; as a Christian, he regarded them as horrible demons. He also showed that his own brand of Christianity could be cruel, for he tortured and burned alive an Aztec chief for supposed blasphemy.

In the middle of this uneasy situation, Cortés was forced to return to the coast and fight off his Spanish enemies. While he was gone, his deputy Alvarado, massacred a crowd of Aztecs whom he believed were about to attack. When Cortés returned to Tenochtitlán he found the Spaniards besieged in their palace. When Montezuma tried to speak to his people, he was stoned and later died. It was war at last.

Above *Cortés and his Spanish troops were all Catholics, who believed in one God. They were horrified that the Aztecs worshiped so many different gods and sacrificed humans to them. So they started to pull down temples and pagan statues in Tenochtitlán.*

War!

Below *War soon broke out between the Spaniards and the Aztecs. The Spaniards were heavily outnumbered and decided to break out of Tenochtitlán. Many were killed as they fought their way to freedom across the causeway. The Spaniards called the retreat "Noche Triste," or Sad Night.*

Trapped in the city, the Spaniards were soon in difficulties. Cortés had brought reinforcements up from the coast, but his men were still hopelessly outnumbered. Their horses were of little use in the barricaded streets and canals of Tenochtitlán, and they had to face wave after wave of frontal attacks combined with showers of arrows fired down on them from the rooftops. Many Aztecs were killed, but they could afford heavy losses. The Spaniards, with a mounting casualty list, could not.

Cortés now realized that there was no choice: the Spaniards must retreat. One night, eight months after their triumphant arrival, they tried to escape in secret along one of the causeways that linked Tenochtitlán with

the mainland.

The Aztecs were waiting for them. The retreat became a disaster which the Spaniards afterwards called "Noche Triste" — the Sad Night. A dense mass of warriors made them fight every inch of the way, while men in hundreds of canoes attacked them on both sides of the causeway. Many Spaniards, loaded down with gold they had been too greedy to leave behind, sank under their own weight when they fell into the lake or tried to swim to safety.

Cortés and a few hundred men managed to fight their way through. Day after day as they fled, the Aztecs harried them. But then the Aztecs decided to give up their guerrilla tactics and fight a pitched battle against the Spaniards, not realizing that in open fields the Spanish horses would be as effective as tanks. At Otumba, the Aztec army was slaughtered. The Spaniards were saved, and their luck had turned.

The destruction of the Aztecs

Above *A gruesome figure of Mixtantecutli, god of death.*

Cortés and his men reached the safety of Tlaxcala and began to prepare a counterattack. Reinforcements arrived at just the right time from Spain, and many Indian tribes that hated Aztec rule now sent contingents to swell the Spanish-led army.

Cortés did not attack Tenochtitlán at once. Instead, he marched round the lake in which it stood, methodically capturing one Aztec town after another until the capital was isolated. Meanwhile he built thirteen small sailing ships — sloops — for action on the lake itself.

The siege of Tenochtitlán was a bloodbath. The Spaniards and their allies advanced down the causeway while their sloops destroyed hundreds of Aztec canoes and took command of the lake. But the Aztecs, now led by a new emperor, Cuauhtémoc, fought desperately. They defended the causeways, then fell back into the city, where they contested every street.

Spanish progress was slow, but two factors doomed the Aztecs. One was their way of fighting: to the very end, they wasted effort in trying to capture Spaniards for sacrifice instead of killing them when they had the chance. The other factor was the Spaniards' Indian allies. At the height of the campaign they numbered at least 150,000, and without them the Spaniards could not have cut off Tenochtitlán from the mainland.

Even so, the siege lasted over three months. Finally, on August 13, 1521, the last Aztec strongpoint was stormed and its fifteen thousand defenders were slaughtered. Cuauhtémoc fled in a canoe but was caught and later hanged.

Opposite *In 1521 Cortés besieged Tenochtitlán with a large army of Indian allies and reinforcements from Spain. After three months of ferocious fighting the Aztecs, under their new emperor Cuauhtémoc, were defeated.*

7 THE MEXICAN HERITAGE

With the fall of Tenochtitlán, Aztec resistance came to an end. The surviving Aztecs — and their Indian enemies as well — became subjects of Spain, and their ancient way of life was quickly destroyed. Tenochtitlán itself was razed to the ground on the orders of Cortés, who built a new Spanish city, Mexico City, on the site. Temples were destroyed, images of the gods were smashed, and the Indians were converted to Christianity by force. Most Aztec books and many of their treasures perished; much of their gold and silver work, for example, was melted down to pay the debts of Cortés's master, the Emperor Charles V.

The Indians themselves suffered terribly. Huge numbers died of European diseases against which their bodies had not built up immunities. Most of those who survived became the slaves of Spanish settlers, despite the good intentions of the government in distant Europe and the noble efforts of some priests and friars. Conditions did eventually improve but by that time there was almost nothing left of Aztec civilization.

However, millions of Mexicans still speak the Aztecs' language, Nahuatl, and the Aztecs' obsession with blood, skulls and death seems to have left some mark on their descendants. On the second of November every year, Mexicans put on skull masks and celebrate a "Day of the Dead" with music and dancing. They even send sugar skulls as presents to children!

Mexico, like the rest of Spain's vast empire in Central and South America, won its independence in the early nineteenth century. Today, Mexicans are proud of their Aztec past, and it is Cuauhtémoc, and not Cortés, who is a national hero.

Above and
Opposite *Hernán Cortés; Montezuma; a glyph of Quetzalcoatl; picture writing from a ritual calendar; a Jaguar Knight; Spaniards destroying Aztec statues; and an Aztec temple where human sacrifices took place.*

Table of dates

c **BC 1200** The emergence of the first Central American civilization: the Olmec culture, centerd on the Gulf of Mexico, southeast of Mexico City.

c **100 BC-AD 1200** This period saw the rise and fall of several Central American civilizations, including the Maya in what is now Guatemala, and the Toltec Empire in the Valley of Mexico.

c **1250-1325** Aztecs appear in the Valley of Mexico. Aztecs start building the city of Tenochtitlán, on an island in Lake Texcoco.

1428 Triple alliance of Tenochtitlán, Texcoco, and Tlacopan overthrows the Tepanec Empire. Beginning of Aztec greatness, under the chief Itzcoatl.

1440-68 Reign of Montezuma I, greatest of Aztec conquerors.

1490s Aztec Empire reaches its greatest extent.

1492 Christopher Columbus explores the islands of the Caribbean.

1503 Montezuma II becomes emperor of the Aztecs.

1519 Hernán Cortés, a Spanish soldier, reaches the mainland of Central America.
Cortés marches inland (August).
The Spaniards enter Tenochtitlán (November 8).

1520 Montezuma is killed.
"Noche Triste": the Spaniards' flight from Tenochtitlán.

1521 Siege of Tenochtitlán begins (May).
Tenochtitlán falls to the Spaniards: the end of the Aztec Empire.

New words

Adobe Sun-dried mud bricks, used by the Aztecs and many other peoples to build houses.

Almanac A book containing information that relates to the calendar.

Atlatl A wooden spear-thrower.

Barter To exchange goods without any money payment.

Blasphemy Words or acts that show great disrespect for God.

Cacao bean Bean of the cacao plant, used by the Aztecs to make drinking chocolate. The Spaniards brought chocolate to Europe, but hard, eating chocolate was not invented until the nineteenth century.

Civil servants People who deal with the everyday running of government business.

Clan Aztec towns were divided into "clans." Each clan gave out land, collected taxes, and enforced law and order within its own area.

Guerrilla A method of fighting in which an army is harassed by small bands of men.

Hostage A person who is held captive as a guarantee that promises made by an enemy will be carried out.

Imperial Something connected with an empire, e.g. an imperial palace is the palace where the emperor lives.

Jade A semi-precious stone, usually green in color, much prized by the Aztecs.

Land reclamation The process of turning useless land (often under water) into land that can support dwellings or grow crops.

Litter A large wooden frame carried on the shoulders of a number of men, used to transport the emperor.

Musket A gun with a long barrel, used before the rifle was invented.

Obsidian Volcanic glass-like rock used to make spearheads and blades for clubs.

Pochteca Aztec merchants who were also trained to spy on the peoples they traded with.

Pulque An alcoholic drink made from the fermented juice of the maguey cactus. Mexicans still drink it.

Quetzal A bird of the pheasant family. Its beautiful feathers were worn by the emperor and the most important nobles.

Scribe A professional writer who recorded events using the Aztec picture words (glyphs).

Telpochcalli The school where boys trained as warriors.

Vassal A person who had the use of land belonging to an overlord and was therefore obliged to serve him.

Further information

Places to visit

Museums. To help you in your study of the Aztecs, there are many excellent museums in the United States. A good place to start is the Museum of the American Indian in New York City.

But there is no museum to match the National Museum of Anthropology in Mexico City for Aztec studies. Besides authentic objects, there are excellent models and plans that give a convincing picture of what life was like in Aztec times.

Famous sites. The great Aztec city of Tenochtitlán was destroyed by the Spaniards, who built their own capital, Mexico City, on the same spot. Elsewhere, they also demolished the majority of the Aztecs' temples. So only a few smaller sites remain, Tenayuca in Mexico City, Zempoala in the state of Veracruz, Malinalco in Oaxaca, and Teopanzolco in the town of Cuernavaca. Although it takes a lively imagination to picture them in all their original splendor, they are well worth visiting.

The cities and temples of earlier Central American peoples were very like the Aztecs' and are much better preserved. Teotihuacan in the state of Mexico, and the Mayan ruins of Chichen Itza in Yucatan state, are particularly famous.

Books

Beck, Barbara L. *The Aztecs, revised edition.* New York: Franklin Watts, 1983.

Collis, Maurice. *Cortez and Montezuma.* New York: Avon, 1978.

Crosher, Judith, et al. *The Aztecs.* Morristown, NJ: Silver Burdett, 1977.

Dorner, Jane. *Cortés and the Aztecs.* New York: Longman, 1972.

Karen, Ruth. *Feathered Serpent: The Rise and Fall of the Aztecs.* New York: Scholastic Inc./Four Winds, 1979.

Lewis, Brenda R. *Growing Up in Aztec Times.* North Pomfret, VT: David & Charles, 1981.

Purdy, Susan and Cass R. Sandak. *Aztecs.* New York: Franklin Watts, 1982.

Wilkes, John. *Hernán Cortés: Conquistador in Mexico.* Minneapolis, MN: Lerner Publications, 1977.

Index

Picture acknowledgments

The illustrations in this book were supplied by: BBC Hulton Picture Library 11, 40; Mansell Collection 7, 47; Werner Foreman Archive 8, 25, 35, 42, 52, 55.